To: President Trump

Thank you
for
Making America
Great Again!

Follow Hirstified
facebook
instagram
twitter

Guide
through
Trump's
Presidency

by: Hirstified

winning

winning

winning

winning

winning

winning

winning

winning

winning

winning

winning

winning

winning

winning

winning

winning

winning

winning

winning

winning

www.ingramcontent.com/pod-product-compliance
Lightning Source LLC
Chambersburg PA
CBHW030013040426
42337CB00012BA/772